# THE L OOK OF

# BI

# TIP



MEG AVENT

# THE LITTLE BOOK OF BISCUIT TIPS

MEG AVENT

A.
Absolute Press

First published in Great Britain in 2013 by
**Absolute Press,** an imprint of Bloomsbury Publishing Plc
Scarborough House, 29 James Street West
Bath BA1 2BT, England
**Phone** +44 (0)1225 316013 **Fax** +44 (0)1225 445836
**E-mail** info@absolutepress.co.uk
**Web** www.absolutepress.co.uk



A catalogue record of this book is available from the British Library
**ISBN 13: 9781906650902**
Printed and bound by Hung Hing, China.

Bloomsbury Publishing Plc
50 Bedford Square, London WC1B 3DP I www.bloomsbury.com

‘Run, run as fast as you can;
You can’t catch me,
I’m the Gingerbread Man.’

**First published in 1875 in**
***St. Nicholas Magazine***

# 1

Biscuits spread while baking. As a general rule, space unbaked biscuits about 5cm apart on the baking tray **to allow room for them to spread** as they bake.

# 2

**Keep your biscuits nice and fresh** by placing them in an airtight container, preferably a tin, where they should keep fresh and in tip-top condition for up to a week.

# 3

**The easiest method for crushing biscuits:** place in a strong plastic food bag and bash hard with a rolling pin. Perfect for cheesecake bases and great as a stress buster too!

# 4

You don't necessarily need special biscuit dough cutters, just

# cut out your own template

from an old cereal packet, place on to your rolled-out dough and use a sharp knife to cut around.

# 5

To prevent biscuits from becoming hard and tough, **avoid using too much flour on your surface** whilst rolling out your dough.

# 6

For uniformly baked biscuits you need evenly rolled dough; **use rolling pin guides** to roll your dough to an even thickness.

# 7

A dark baking sheet will conduct heat better than a light one. If using dark sheets, bake for slightly less time **to avoid brown bottoms!**

# 8

When cooking a large number of biscuits

**take care to cool your baking sheet between batches.** A hot sheet will melt the dough before it reaches the oven and will result in it not baking correctly.

# 9

However rigorously you follow a recipe, all ovens are different and baking times will differ, so,

**watch your biscuits closely,**

especially in the last few minutes.

# 10

**Use a pancake turner** to help avoid your biscuits becoming misshapen when being transferred to the sheet for baking.

# 11

# Never overlap your biscuits

on the cooling wire rack, or you risk them becoming soggy!

# 12

**Biscuits have become too hard?** Pop a slice of bread into the tin to slightly soften them.

# 13

# Easy crackers for cheese

– combine 200g of flour, 1 teaspoon of baking powder 50g of butter and a little water. Roll out, cut into squares and sprinkle with salt, fennel seeds or sesame seeds. Bake for 10 minutes.

# 14

**Biscuits freeze well for up to 3 months.** Just place in an airtight container, separate layers with greaseproof paper and place in the freezer.

# 15

# If you are decorating with royal icing

it's best to wait a day after baking as this will help prevent any oil in the biscuit leaching into the icing.

# 16

Why not **freeze individual biscuits** for lunchboxes?

They'll be defrosted by lunchtime!

# 17

Invest in some **silicone baking mats;**

they are reusable, last forever, don't need greasing and are even dishwasher-friendly!

# 18

**Never store your cakes and biscuits together,** as the moisture in the sponge will make your biscuits soggy.

# 19

# Refresh previously baked biscuits

by heating them in a low oven for 5 minutes.

# 20

# A truly delectable dessert biscuit

has to be the brandy snap: dip in melted dark chocolate, fill with whipped cream and serve with syllabub.

# 21

# Stick closely to the recipe.

Even adding a larger sized egg than is called for could result in tough biscuits.

# 22

You can **create great biscuits for vegan friends**

by substituting soya fat for butter in your recipe.

# 23

If your biscuit **dough appears too wet** don't immediately add more flour. Let it rest for 30 minutes and then decide.

# 24

# Don't rush!

Freshly baked **biscuits need to rest**

on the baking tray for a few minutes before lifting them. This allows them to set.

# 25

For perfectly shaped biscuits;

**dust your cutters with flour** to prevent them from sticking to the dough.

26

**If** you're **cutting out large and particularly delicate shapes,** roll and cut out your dough onto baking parchment and then slide directly onto the baking sheet.

# 27

**For a quick glaze for sweet biscuits,** beat one egg white until just frothy, brush over unbaked biscuits, sprinkle with caster sugar and bake.

# 28

# Add extra decorations before your icing sets.

How about trying desiccated coconut, toasted almonds, chocolate buttons, and dragées?

# 29

**Don't be too hasty** in moving royal-iced biscuits – they need to stand for at least 2 hours before you can move them safely.

# 30

Even just a little warmth will ruin a wonderful crunch, so **allow biscuits to cool completely** before storing.

# 31

For an easy, yet impressive look, mix some chocolate dough and some vanilla dough, press together and roll and cut out

**to form a marble effect.**

# 32

A plastic squeezable bottle with a small nozzle

**makes** the task of

**icing batches of biscuits much easier**

than using a number of paper piping bags.

# 33

Sugar paste makes **a quick, easy and neat icing** for your biscuits.

Use any colour, roll and cut out to 4mm thick. Stick the icing onto the biscuit with boiled apricot jam.

# 34

Using royal icing, pipe a thin line round the perimeter of your baked biscuit, then thin the icing with a little water and 'flood' the area within to **create an impressive glossy iced biscuit.**

# 35

To make stunning Christmas biscuits, cut the dough into Christmas tree shapes and place on a lined baking sheet. Cut out 2 small circles and fill with crushed red or green boiled sweets to

**produce a stained-glass effect** when baked.

# 36

**Dunking is a controversial subject!** The much-loved ginger nut probably produces the best dunk, but for a faster dunk choose a digestive. For a long, slow dunk, it has to be biscotti.

# 37

To make a lovely

**homemade wedding favour;** ice your biscuits and pipe each guest's name on. Place in a cellophane bag and tie with coordinating ribbon.

# 38

**If a good snap**

is what you desire: more sugar and less butter.

**If chewiness**

is what you love: more butter and less sugar.

# 39

No chocolate chips in your storecupboard?

Just **smash some cooking chocolate into pieces.** You'll get a more rustic look but your biscuits will be just as delicious.

# 40

A very soft and sticky cookie mixture is much

**easier** handled **with**

vinyl **disposable**

**catering gloves.**

# 41

Almond Florentines make

# perfect gluten-free celebration biscuits.

You can even make the mixture a few days ahead and leave in the fridge until needed.

# 42

Cold eggs can cause the mix to contract and become tough –

**always have your eggs at room temperature.**

# 43

# For simple buttermilk biscuits that children will love,

preheat the oven to 180°C.

Mix together 40g of rolled oats, 100g of plain flour, $^{1}/_{4}$ teaspoon of bicarbonate of soda and $^{1}/_{4}$ teaspoon of salt. Rub in 55g of butter. Stir in 60ml buttermilk and 2 teaspoons of honey to form a stiff dough. Roll out to 3mm thick, cut out and bake for 7 minutes.

# 44

The path to successful baking starts with very accurate measures. **Invest in a set of digital scales.**

45

Use cocktail sticks for testing

**to see if your dough is cooked.** Any mixture left on the stick indicates your biscuits need a couple more minutes in the oven.

46

**For an easy last-minute decoration,** sift some icing sugar over your biscuit using a tea strainer.

47

# Prevent extra spreading whilst baking

by always chilling freshly made dough in the fridge for about an hour before you roll and cut out.

# 48

**For chewy, cookie-like biscuits,** very slightly under-bake and allow for the heat to continue cooking them for a few more minutes after leaving the oven.

# 49

**For easy gluten-free peanut butter cookies,** preheat the oven to 180°C. Cream together 125g of butter and 175g of soft brown sugar. Beat in 125g of peanut butter and 1 egg. Mix in 1 teaspoon of baking powder and 17g of rice flour. Roll teaspoon-sized balls and place on baking sheet. Flatten with a fork. Bake for 15 minutes.

# 50

A few sugar cubes placed inside the tin in which you store your biscuits will soak up any moisture, ensuring your **biscuits maintain their crispness.**

# Meg Avent

Through her work in cookery book publishing, Meg has commissioned some of the country's leading patisserie chefs. Inspired by their work, and having always had a passion for cake decorating, she went on to train at one of London's leading cake companies. After running her own company for a number of years she now enjoys baking for family and friends.

THE LITTLE BOOK OF
BARBECUE
TIPS
ANDREW LANGLEY

THE LITTLE BOOK OF
BEER
TIPS
ANDREW LANGLEY

THE LITTLE BOOK OF
HERB
TIPS
WILLIAM FORTT

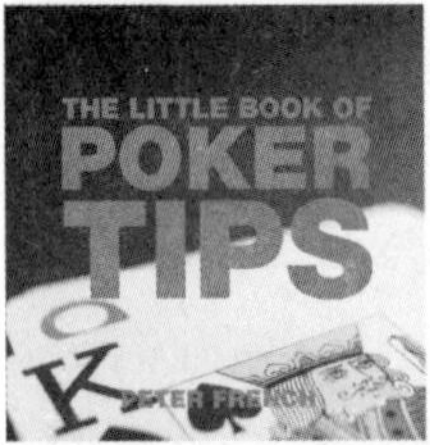
THE LITTLE BOOK OF
POKER
TIPS

THE LITTLE BOOK OF
GARDENING
TIPS
WILLIAM FORTT

THE LITTLE BOOK OF
CHEFS'
TIPS
RICHARD MAGGS

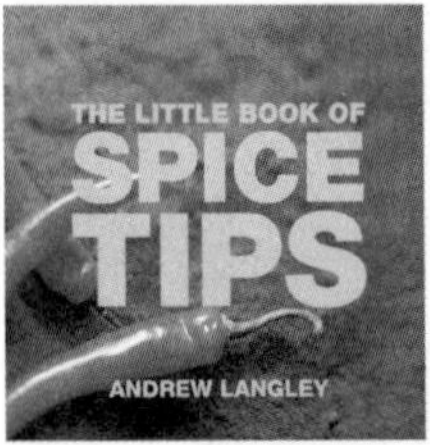
THE LITTLE BOOK OF
SPICE
TIPS
ANDREW LANGLEY

THE LITTLE BOOK OF
GOLF
TIPS
PETER FRENCH

THE LITTLE BOOK OF
TIPS
SERIES

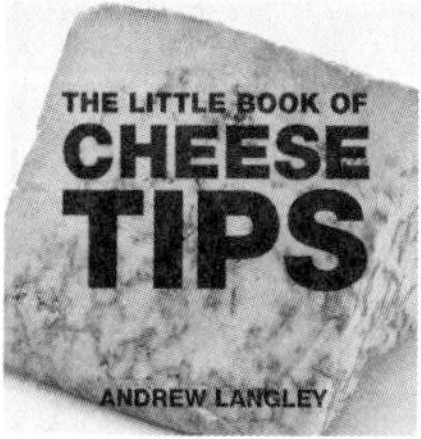
THE LITTLE BOOK OF
CHEESE
TIPS
ANDREW LANGLEY

THE LITTLE BOOK OF
WINE
TIPS
ANDREW LANGLEY

THE LITTLE BOOK OF
AGA
TIPS$^{2}$
RICHARD MAGGS

THE LITTLE BOOK OF
COFFEE
TIPS
ANDREW LANGLEY

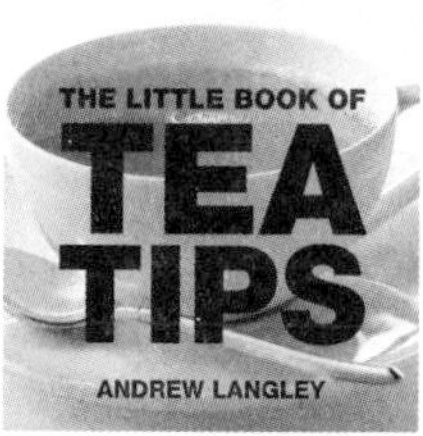
THE LITTLE BOOK OF
TEA
TIPS
ANDREW LANGLEY

THE LITTLE BOOK OF
AGA
TIPS$^{3}$
RICHARD MAGGS

THE LITTLE BOOK OF
AGA
TIPS
RICHARD MAGGS

THE LITTLE BOOK OF
CHRISTMAS
AGA
TIPS
RICHARD MAGGS

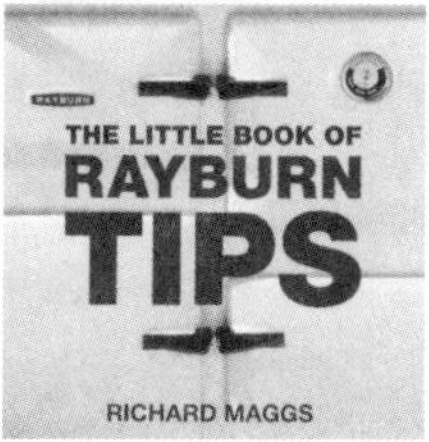
THE LITTLE BOOK OF
RAYBURN
TIPS
RICHARD MAGGS

THE LITTLE BOOK OF
BRIDGE
TIPS
PETER FRENCH

THE LITTLE BOOK OF
CHESS
TIPS
PETER FRENCH

THE LITTLE BOOK OF
FISHING
TIPS

THE LITTLE BOOK OF
GREEN
TIPS
WILLIAM FORTT

THE LITTLE BOOK OF
KITTEN
TIPS
ANDREW LANGLEY

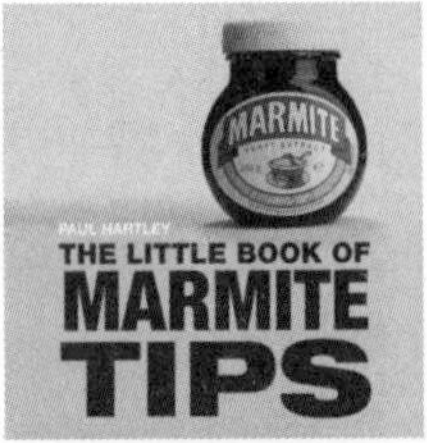
MARMITE
PAUL HARTLEY
THE LITTLE BOOK OF
MARMITE
TIPS

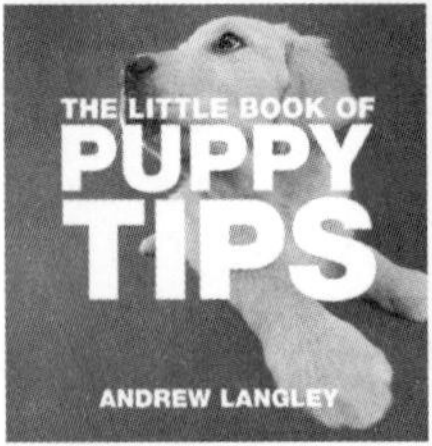
THE LITTLE BOOK OF
PUPPY
TIPS
ANDREW LANGLEY

THE LITTLE BOOK OF
WHISKY
TIPS
ANDREW LANGLEY

THE LITTLE BOOK OF
TRAVEL
TIPS
MEGAN DEVENISH

# Little Books of Tips from Absolute Press

Aga Tips
Aga Tips 2
Aga Tips 3
Allotment Tips
Backgammon Tips
Barbecue Tips
Beer Tips
Biscuit Tips
Bread Tips
Bridge Tips
Cake Baking Tips
Cake Decorating Tips
Cheese Tips
Chefs' Tips
Chess Tips
Chocolate Tips
Christmas Aga Tips
Chutney and Pickle Tips
Cleaning Tips
Cocktail Tips
Coffee Tips
Cupcake Tips
Curry Tips
Fishing Tips
Fly Fishing Tips
Frugal Tips
Gardening Tips
Golf Tips
Green Tips
Grow Your Own Tips
Herb Tips
Houseplant Tips
Ice Cream Tips
Jam Tips
Kitten Tips
Macaroon Tips
Marmite Tips
Olive Oil Tips
Pasta Tips
Poker Tips
Puppy Tips
Rayburn Tips
Seafood Tips
Spice Tips
Tea Tips
Toast Tips
Travel Tips
Whisky Tips
Wine Tips
Vinegar Tips